Gatlinburg Travel Guide 2024-2025

Your Exclusive Guide to Planning the Perfect and Budget-Friendly Vacation

Nancy B. Bacher

Disclaimer

This travel guide is intended to provide helpful and informative material on the subjects addressed. It is not intended to be a substitute for professional advice or guidance. The author and publisher have made every effort to ensure the accuracy of the information herein; however, they assume no responsibility for errors, omissions, or contrary interpretation of the subject matter.

The information provided is on an "as is" basis and the author and publisher make no representations or warranties of any kind with respect to the completeness or accuracy of the contents. All travel plans should be verified with the appropriate authorities and professionals. The author and publisher shall not be liable for any loss or damage allegedly arising from any information or suggestions contained in this book.

Travel conditions and guidelines are subject to change, and travelers are encouraged to stay informed and make decisions based on current conditions and personal circumstances.

Contents

Chapter 1: Planning Your Trip

Setting Your Travel Goals

Setting your travel goals is the foundation of a successful and fulfilling trip. Whether you're an adventurer seeking thrilling experiences, a nature enthusiast yearning to explore the great outdoors, or a culture buff eager to delve into local traditions, clearly defining your goals will shape your entire travel experience. Start by asking yourself what you hope to achieve and experience on your trip to

Gatlinburg. Are you looking for relaxation, adventure, or a mix of both? Understanding your desires will help you prioritize activities and destinations.

Consider the purpose of your trip. Are you traveling solo, with family, or friends? Each scenario might require different plans and considerations. For instance, family trips might focus on kid-friendly activities, while solo travelers might seek more introspective and personalized experiences.

Another essential aspect of setting your travel goals is determining your budget. Knowing how much you're willing to spend will influence your choices regarding accommodation, dining, and activities. It's helpful to categorize your budget into sections such as lodging, food, transportation, and entertainment. This way, you can allocate funds appropriately and avoid overspending.

Your travel goals should also include a timeframe. How long do you plan to stay in Gatlinburg? A clear timeline allows you to structure your itinerary effectively, ensuring you make the most of your visit without feeling rushed. For example, a weekend trip might focus on a few key attractions, while a week-long stay could accommodate more in-depth exploration.

Lastly, think about any specific interests or hobbies you want to pursue. Gatlinburg offers a plethora of activities, from hiking in the Great Smoky Mountains to visiting museums and enjoying local cuisine. Identifying your interests beforehand will help you tailor your trip to include activities that genuinely excite you.

Setting clear travel goals not only enhances your trip planning but also ensures that your experience in Gatlinburg is meaningful and aligned with your desires. It's about creating a journey that reflects your passions and provides lasting memories. Take the time to reflect on what you want from your trip, and let those goals guide your planning process.

Research and Resources

Thorough research is crucial for a well-planned and enjoyable trip to Gatlinburg. With the right resources, you can uncover hidden gems, avoid common pitfalls, and make informed decisions that enhance your travel experience. Start by exploring official tourism websites, such as the Gatlinburg Convention and Visitors Bureau, which offer a wealth of information on attractions, events, accommodations, and dining options.

Travel blogs and forums are excellent resources for personal insights and recommendations. Websites like TripAdvisor, Lonely Planet, and Reddit provide user-generated content where travelers share their experiences, tips, and reviews. These platforms can help you gauge popular attractions, discover off-the-beaten-path activities, and find honest opinions on accommodations and restaurants.

Guidebooks are another valuable resource, offering curated content and expert advice. Titles like "Fodor's The Complete Guide to the National Parks of the USA" and "Moon Great Smoky Mountains National Park" provide in-depth information about Gatlinburg and its surroundings. They often include detailed maps, itineraries, and practical tips that can enhance your planning process.

Social media platforms such as Instagram and Pinterest are also great for discovering travel inspiration. Search for hashtags like #Gatlinburg or #GreatSmokyMountains to find stunning photos, travel stories, and recommendations. Follow travel influencers and local businesses to stay updated on current trends and events.

Don't underestimate the power of local knowledge. Reach out to friends, family, or acquaintances who have visited Gatlinburg. Their firsthand experiences can provide valuable insights and personalized recommendations. Additionally, consider contacting local tourism offices or visitor centers for brochures, maps, and expert advice.

Apps like Google Maps and Yelp are indispensable tools for navigating Gatlinburg and finding the best places to eat, shop, and explore. Google Maps offers detailed directions, real-time traffic updates, and user reviews, while Yelp provides comprehensive reviews and ratings for restaurants, shops, and attractions.

Finally, consider joining travel groups or online communities focused on Gatlinburg. These groups often share tips, itineraries, and special deals. Engaging with fellow travelers can provide a sense of camaraderie and additional insights that might not be available through traditional research methods.

By leveraging these resources, you can create a well-rounded travel plan that covers all aspects of your trip. Thorough research ensures that you make informed decisions, maximize your time, and have a memorable and enjoyable experience in Gatlinburg.

Travel Insurance

Travel insurance is a crucial yet often overlooked component of trip planning. It provides a safety net against unexpected events that could otherwise disrupt your travel plans and result in significant financial losses. Understanding the importance and benefits of travel insurance can help ensure a smooth and worry-free trip to Gatlinburg.

Firstly, travel insurance covers trip cancellations and interruptions. Unforeseen circumstances such as illness, family emergencies, or natural disasters can force you to cancel or cut short your trip. With travel insurance, you can recover non-refundable expenses like airfare, hotel bookings, and tour reservations, minimizing your financial loss.

Medical emergencies can happen anytime, and having travel insurance ensures you are covered for unexpected health issues. Most travel insurance policies include coverage for medical expenses, hospitalization, and emergency evacuation. This is particularly important if you plan to engage in outdoor activities like hiking or skiing in Gatlinburg, where the risk of injury might be higher.

Lost or delayed luggage can be a significant inconvenience, especially when you're away from home. Travel insurance often includes coverage for lost, stolen, or damaged baggage, as well as compensation for essential items if your luggage is delayed. This can help you replace necessary belongings and continue your trip with minimal disruption.

Travel insurance also provides coverage for travel delays. If your flight is delayed or canceled due to weather, mechanical issues, or other reasons, travel insurance can reimburse you for additional expenses like meals, accommodation, and transportation incurred during the delay.

When selecting a travel insurance policy, it's important to read the fine print and understand what is covered and any exclusions. Policies vary, so compare different options to find one that suits your needs. Consider factors like the duration of your trip, planned activities, and personal health conditions.

In addition to standard coverage, some travel insurance policies offer additional benefits such as rental car insurance, accidental death and dismemberment coverage, and 24/7 assistance services. These extras can provide further peace of mind and support during your trip.

Purchasing travel insurance is relatively easy. Many companies offer online quotes and instant coverage. Compare different providers and policies to find the best fit for your trip to Gatlinburg. Consider reading reviews and seeking recommendations to ensure you choose a reputable provider.

In conclusion, travel insurance is an essential investment that protects you from unforeseen events and provides financial and medical security. It allows you to travel with confidence, knowing that you are covered in case of emergencies. Make travel insurance a priority in your trip planning to Gatlinburg, and enjoy a worry-free and memorable journey.

Packing Tips and Tricks

Packing for a trip can be a daunting task, but with some strategic planning and useful tips, you can make it a hassle-free experience. Proper packing ensures that you have everything you need without overburdening yourself with unnecessary items. Here are some essential packing tips and tricks for your trip to Gatlinburg.

Start by creating a packing list. This helps you stay organized and ensures you don't forget important items. Divide your list into categories such as clothing, toiletries, electronics, and travel documents. Consider the weather and activities planned for your trip to tailor your list accordingly.

Choose versatile clothing. Opt for items that can be mixed and matched to create different outfits. Pack layers, as the weather in Gatlinburg can be unpredictable, especially in the mountains. Lightweight, moisture-wicking clothing is ideal for outdoor activities, while a warm jacket and comfortable shoes are essential for cooler temperatures and hiking.

Roll your clothes instead of folding them. Rolling saves space and minimizes wrinkles. Use packing cubes to keep your belongings organized and easily accessible. These cubes also help compress your clothing, creating more room in your suitcase.

Limit the number of shoes you bring. Choose a few pairs that are comfortable and suitable for various activities. A good rule of thumb is to pack one pair of walking shoes, one pair of casual shoes, and one pair of dressier shoes if needed.

Utilize travel-sized toiletries. Purchase small containers or use refillable bottles to bring only the amount you need. This saves space and complies with airline liquid restrictions. Pack toiletries in a separate, leak-proof bag to prevent spills.

Don't forget essential electronics and their chargers. If you plan to take photos, bring extra memory cards or a portable storage device. A power bank can be invaluable for keeping your devices charged while on the go.

Pack a small first-aid kit with basic medical supplies such as band-aids, pain relievers, and any prescription medications you may need. It's also wise to include items like insect repellent and sunscreen, especially if you plan to spend time outdoors.

Consider the type of luggage that best suits your trip. A sturdy, lightweight suitcase with wheels is ideal for most travelers. If you plan to hike or engage in outdoor activities, a durable backpack may be more appropriate. Ensure your luggage is easily identifiable with a luggage tag and a unique marker.

Keep important documents such as your ID, passport, travel insurance, and itinerary in a secure, easily accessible place. Consider using a travel wallet or document organizer to keep everything together.

Lastly, pack a reusable water bottle and snacks. Staying hydrated and having quick access to food can make your travels more comfortable and enjoyable.

By following these packing tips and tricks, you can ensure that you have everything you need for your trip to Gatlinburg while keeping your luggage manageable and organized. Proper packing allows you to focus on enjoying your adventure without the stress of forgetting essential items.

Chapter 2: When to Visit

Seasonal Weather Patterns

Gatlinburg, nestled in the Great Smoky Mountains, experiences distinct seasonal weather patterns that can greatly influence your travel plans. Understanding these patterns will help you decide the best time to visit based on your preferences and planned activities.

- Spring (March to May): Spring in Gatlinburg is characterized by mild temperatures, ranging from the mid-50s to the low 70s°F. This season is marked by blooming wildflowers and lush greenery, making it an ideal time for hiking and exploring the natural beauty of the Smokies. However, spring can also bring unpredictable weather, including occasional rain showers and cool mornings and evenings, so packing layers is advisable.

- Summer (June to August): Summers in Gatlinburg are warm and humid, with temperatures typically ranging from the mid-70s to the high 80s°F. This is the peak season for family vacations, as the weather is perfect for outdoor activities such as hiking, rafting, and enjoying local attractions. Afternoon thunderstorms are common, so it's wise to carry a rain jacket or umbrella. The lush foliage and vibrant greenery make the mountains particularly scenic during this time.

- Fall (September to November): Fall is one of the most popular times to visit Gatlinburg, thanks to the stunning autumn foliage. Temperatures are generally comfortable, ranging from the mid-50s to the low 70s°F. The changing colors of the leaves attract many visitors, especially during October. Fall is also harvest season, offering opportunities to enjoy local festivals and events. Be prepared for cooler temperatures in the mornings and evenings, and potentially crowded trails and attractions.

- Winter (December to February): Winters in Gatlinburg are relatively mild compared to other parts of the country, with temperatures ranging from the mid-30s to the low 50s°F. While snow is possible, it is not guaranteed, making winter a quieter and more peaceful time to visit. This season is ideal for those looking to enjoy the holiday festivities and the charm of a mountain town adorned with lights and decorations. Skiing and snowboarding are available at nearby Ober Gatlinburg, though snowfall can be sporadic.

Each season in Gatlinburg offers unique experiences and scenic beauty. By understanding the seasonal weather patterns, you can choose the best time to visit based on your weather preferences and the activities you wish to enjoy.

Peak Tourist Seasons

Gatlinburg, with its picturesque landscapes and numerous attractions, sees fluctuations in tourist numbers throughout the year. Knowing the peak tourist seasons can help you plan your trip to avoid crowds or take advantage of bustling energy and events.

Summer (June to August): Summer is the peak tourist season in Gatlinburg. Families flock to the area during school vacations, drawn by the warm weather and outdoor activities. Attractions like Dollywood, Ripley's Aquarium, and the Great Smoky Mountains National Park are bustling with visitors. Accommodations and popular spots can get crowded, and prices for hotels and attractions are typically higher. Booking well in advance is recommended if you plan to visit during this time.

Fall (September to November): Fall is another peak season, particularly from late September to early November, when the autumn foliage is at its most vibrant. The spectacular display of colors attracts leaf-peepers from all over the country. The Great Smoky Mountains National Park is especially busy during this period, with heavy traffic on popular scenic drives and trails. Festivals and events celebrating the harvest season also draw large crowds. As with summer, early booking is crucial to secure accommodations and preferred activities.

Spring Break (March to April): Although not as crowded as summer and fall, spring break sees a significant increase in visitors, particularly families and college students. The pleasant weather and blooming flowers make it an attractive time for outdoor activities. Popular attractions can experience higher foot traffic, and prices may rise slightly during this period.

Holiday Season (December): The holiday season, especially around Christmas and New Year's, sees a spike in tourists. Gatlinburg's festive decorations, holiday events, and winter activities like skiing and ice skating at Ober Gatlinburg draw visitors looking for a cozy, festive getaway. While not as busy as summer and fall, it's still wise to book accommodations and activities in advance.

Off-Peak Periods: The off-peak periods, particularly in late winter (January to February) and early spring (early March), offer a quieter, more relaxed experience. These times are ideal for those who prefer fewer crowds and potentially lower prices. While the weather may be cooler, the tranquility and lower rates can make for an appealing visit.

Understanding Gatlinburg's peak tourist seasons helps you plan your visit to either join in the vibrant hustle or find solace in quieter times, depending on your preference.

Best Times for Specific Activities

The diverse offerings of Gatlinburg make it a year-round destination, but certain times of the year are better suited for specific activities. Knowing the best times for your preferred activities can help you maximize your enjoyment and experiences.

- Hiking and Outdoor Adventures: Spring (March to May) and fall (September to November) are ideal for hiking and exploring the Great Smoky Mountains National Park. In spring, the trails are adorned with blooming wildflowers, while fall offers stunning autumn foliage. Temperatures during these seasons are mild, providing comfortable hiking conditions. Popular trails include Alum Cave, Chimney Tops, and Laurel Falls. Early morning hikes are recommended to avoid crowds and enjoy cooler temperatures.

- Wildlife Viewing: The best times for wildlife viewing in Gatlinburg are spring and early summer (April to June) and late summer to early fall (August to October). These periods offer increased chances of spotting black bears, elk, deer, and a variety of bird species. Cades Cove and Cataloochee Valley are prime locations for wildlife observation. Early mornings and late afternoons are the best times to see animals as they are most active during these hours.

- Fall Foliage: The peak time for fall foliage in Gatlinburg is typically mid-October to early November. The vibrant colors of the leaves attract many visitors, making it a perfect time for scenic drives, photography, and enjoying the natural beauty of the Smokies. Popular spots for viewing fall colors include Newfound Gap Road, Clingmans Dome, and the Blue Ridge Parkway.

- Skiing and Winter Sports: Winter (December to February) is the best time for skiing, snowboarding, and other winter sports at Ober Gatlinburg. While snowfall can be sporadic, the resort offers snowmaking capabilities to ensure a good base for winter activities. The holiday season also adds a festive atmosphere with decorations and special events.

- Fishing: Spring (April to June) and fall (September to November) are excellent times for fishing in Gatlinburg. The streams in the Great Smoky Mountains National Park are well-stocked with trout, making it a favorite destination for anglers. Licenses are required, and certain streams are designated as catch-and-release only. Early mornings and late afternoons are ideal times for fishing.

- Festivals and Events: Gatlinburg hosts numerous festivals and events throughout the year. The spring and fall seasons are particularly busy with events such as the Spring Wildflower Pilgrimage in April and the Gatlinburg Craftsmen's Fair in July and October. The winter holiday season features the Smoky Mountain Winterfest, which includes Christmas lights, parades, and special holiday activities.

- Whitewater Rafting and Water Activities: Summer (June to August) is the best time for whitewater rafting, tubing, and other water activities. The warmer weather makes it enjoyable to be on the water, and the rivers are typically at a good flow rate. The Pigeon River offers excellent opportunities for rafting and is a popular choice for adventure seekers.

By aligning your travel plans with the best times for your preferred activities, you can ensure a fulfilling and memorable experience in Gatlinburg. Each season offers unique opportunities, allowing you to enjoy the diverse attractions and natural beauty of this charming destination.

Chapter 3: Budgeting for Your Trip

Estimating Costs

Estimating the costs of your Gatlinburg trip involves considering various factors such as accommodation, dining, transportation, activities, and incidental expenses. A well-planned budget can ensure you enjoy your vacation without financial stress.

- Accommodation: The cost of lodging in Gatlinburg varies widely based on the type of accommodation, location, and time of year. Luxury hotels can range from $200 to $500 per night, while mid-range hotels and vacation rentals might cost between $100 and $200 per night. Budget-friendly options, including motels and campgrounds, can be as low as $50 to $100 per night. During peak seasons, prices tend to be higher, so booking in advance is recommended.

- Dining: Dining expenses depend on your preferences and dining choices. For budget travelers, fast food and casual dining options can range from $10 to $20 per meal. Mid-range restaurants typically charge between $20 and $40 per person, while upscale dining experiences can cost $50 or more per person. Consider incorporating some self-catering or picnic meals to save on food costs.

- Transportation: Transportation costs include travel to Gatlinburg and getting around the area. If driving, consider fuel costs, parking fees, and any tolls. For those flying, airfare will vary based on your departure location and the season. Once in Gatlinburg, local transportation options include renting a car, using rideshare services, or taking advantage of the Gatlinburg Trolley, which offers affordable fares for getting around town.

- Activities: Gatlinburg offers a range of activities, from free outdoor adventures to paid attractions. Entrance to the Great Smoky Mountains National Park is free, but other activities like zip-lining, visiting Ripley's Aquarium, or attending shows may have admission fees ranging from $20 to $50 per person. Plan your activities in advance and look for discounts or combination tickets to save money.

- Miscellaneous Expenses: Don't forget to account for incidental expenses such as souvenirs, tips, and any unexpected costs. Setting aside a small buffer in your budget for these items can help you avoid surprises.

By estimating these costs and setting a realistic budget, you can ensure a well-rounded and enjoyable trip to Gatlinburg without overspending.

Money-Saving Tips

Traveling to Gatlinburg doesn't have to break the bank. With some smart planning and a few money-saving strategies, you can enjoy a memorable vacation without overspending.

Travel Off-Peak: One of the best ways to save money is to travel during the off-peak seasons. Visiting Gatlinburg in late winter or early spring can result in significant savings on accommodations and activities, as prices tend to be lower when fewer tourists are around.

Book in Advance: Early booking can secure better rates on hotels and attractions. Many hotels and vacation rentals offer discounts for early reservations. Additionally, booking flights in advance can help you find more affordable airfare.

Look for Discounts and Deals: Take advantage of discounts and deals available online. Websites like Groupon often have discounts on local attractions, dining, and activities. Check the official Gatlinburg tourism website for any current promotions or special offers.

Consider Alternative Accommodations: Instead of staying in a hotel, consider alternative lodging options such as vacation rentals, cabins, or campgrounds. These can often be more cost-effective, especially for families or groups. Additionally, renting a cabin with a kitchen allows you to prepare your meals, saving on dining expenses.

Use the Gatlinburg Trolley: The Gatlinburg Trolley is an affordable way to get around town. With various routes covering popular attractions and points of interest, the trolley can save you money on parking and fuel costs. Day passes are available for unlimited rides, making it a convenient and budget-friendly option.

Take Advantage of Free Activities: Gatlinburg and the surrounding Great Smoky Mountains National Park offer numerous free activities. Enjoy hiking, scenic drives, and wildlife viewing without spending a dime. The park's visitor centers also provide free educational programs and exhibits.

Pack Your Own Snacks and Drinks: Save money on snacks and drinks by packing your own. Bringing a reusable water bottle and refilling it throughout the day can also help you avoid purchasing expensive bottled water.

Eat Smart: To save on dining costs, consider eating out for lunch instead of dinner, as lunch menus are often cheaper. Also, look for restaurants that offer early bird specials or discounts for children. Self-catering some meals can also reduce dining expenses.

Plan Ahead: Create a daily itinerary to avoid impulse spending. Knowing what activities and attractions you want to visit each day can help you stick to your budget and prevent unplanned expenses.

By incorporating these money-saving tips into your travel plans, you can enjoy a fantastic Gatlinburg vacation while keeping your budget intact.

Sample Budget Plans

Creating a budget plan tailored to your travel style can help ensure a stress-free and enjoyable trip to Gatlinburg. Below are sample budget plans for three different travel styles: budget, mid-range, and luxury.

Budget Traveler:

- Accommodation: $50 per night at a budget-friendly motel or campground.
- Dining: $20 per day (breakfast $5, lunch $7, dinner $8) by utilizing fast food, casual dining, and grocery stores.
- Transportation: $20 per day (fuel costs and parking fees if driving or using the Gatlinburg Trolley).
- Activities: $20 per day on affordable attractions and activities, plus free activities like hiking and exploring the Great Smoky Mountains National Park.
- Miscellaneous: $10 per day for souvenirs, tips, and unexpected expenses.

Total Daily Budget: $120

For a 5-day trip, the total budget would be approximately $600.

Mid-Range Traveler:

- Accommodation: $150 per night at a mid-range hotel or vacation rental.
- Dining: $50 per day (breakfast $10, lunch $15, dinner $25) by enjoying a mix of casual and mid-range restaurants.
- Transportation: $30 per day (rental car costs, fuel, and parking fees).
- Activities: $40 per day for a mix of free and paid attractions, including shows, museums, and outdoor activities.
- Miscellaneous: $20 per day for souvenirs, tips, and unexpected expenses.

Total Daily Budget: $290

For a 5-day trip, the total budget would be approximately $1,450.

Luxury Traveler:

- Accommodation: $300 per night at a luxury hotel or upscale cabin.
- Dining: $100 per day (breakfast $20, lunch $30, dinner $50) by dining at upscale restaurants and trying local specialties.
- Transportation: $50 per day (premium rental car, fuel, parking fees, and possibly private transportation services).
- Activities: $100 per day for premium experiences, including guided tours, spa treatments, and exclusive attractions.
- Miscellaneous: $50 per day for high-end souvenirs, tips, and unexpected expenses.

Total Daily Budget: $600

For a 5-day trip, the total budget would be approximately $3,000.

These sample budget plans provide a guideline based on different travel styles. Adjusting the figures according to your preferences and planned activities will help you create a realistic budget that suits your needs. Whether you're traveling on a tight budget or looking for a luxurious getaway, planning your expenses in advance will ensure a smooth and enjoyable trip to Gatlinburg.

Chapter 4: Essentials for Traveling

What to Pack

Packing for a trip to Gatlinburg involves preparing for a variety of activities and weather conditions. Here's a comprehensive guide on what to pack to ensure you're well-prepared for your adventure.

- Clothing: Gatlinburg's weather can vary greatly depending on the season. Pack layers to adapt to changing temperatures. Include comfortable hiking clothes, a waterproof jacket, and sturdy hiking boots if you plan to explore the Great Smoky Mountains National Park. In summer, bring lightweight, breathable clothing and swimwear for water activities. In winter, pack warm clothing, including thermal layers, a hat, gloves, and a heavy coat.

- Footwear: Comfortable, sturdy shoes are essential, especially if you plan on hiking or exploring the outdoors. Consider bringing a pair of sandals or casual shoes for relaxing days in town.

- Accessories: Sunglasses, a hat, and sunscreen are must-haves for sun protection. A reusable water bottle is also important to stay hydrated, especially during outdoor activities. A daypack is useful for carrying essentials while hiking or exploring.

- Toiletries: Pack all necessary toiletries, including travel-sized shampoo, conditioner, toothpaste, and a toothbrush. Don't forget sunscreen, insect repellent, and any prescription medications you may need. A small first aid kit with band-aids, antiseptic wipes, and pain relievers can be handy for minor injuries.

- Electronics: Bring a camera or smartphone to capture the beautiful scenery and memorable moments. Chargers, power banks, and any necessary adapters are essential to keep your devices powered. A pair of binoculars can enhance your wildlife viewing experience.

- Documents: Ensure you have all necessary travel documents, including your ID, travel insurance details, reservation confirmations, and maps. It's also a good idea to have a small amount of cash and credit/debit cards for convenience.

- Specialty Items: Depending on your plans, you might need specific items such as fishing gear, a picnic blanket, or a travel guidebook. If traveling with children, pack items to keep them entertained, such as books, toys, or games.

By packing these essentials, you'll be well-equipped to enjoy your Gatlinburg trip comfortably and safely, no matter what activities you have planned.

Health and Safety Tips

Maintaining health and safety while traveling to Gatlinburg is crucial for an enjoyable trip. Here are some essential tips to keep in mind:

Health Tips:

Stay Hydrated: Drink plenty of water, especially during outdoor activities like hiking. Carry a reusable water bottle and refill it regularly.

- Food Safety: Choose reputable restaurants and eateries to avoid foodborne illnesses. If cooking, ensure food is properly stored and prepared.
- Protect Against the Sun: Use sunscreen with a high SPF, wear hats, and sunglasses to

protect yourself from harmful UV rays, especially when spending extended periods outdoors.

- Medical Needs: Carry a basic first aid kit with band-aids, antiseptic wipes, and any necessary medications. If you have specific medical needs, ensure you have an ample supply of your prescription medications and know the location of nearby pharmacies.

- Allergies: If you have allergies, carry necessary medications such as antihistamines or an epinephrine auto-injector. Inform travel companions about your allergies and know the local emergency services contact information.

Safety Tips:

- Hiking Safety: Always stay on marked trails and carry a map. Inform someone of your plans before heading out. Carry a whistle and a flashlight in case of emergencies.

- Wildlife Awareness: Maintain a safe distance from wildlife. Never feed animals, and store food securely to avoid attracting them. Familiarize yourself with local wildlife and know what to do if you encounter them.
- Weather Preparedness: Check the weather forecast before heading out. Be prepared for sudden weather changes, especially in mountainous areas. During thunderstorms, avoid open fields, high ground, and isolated trees.
- Personal Safety: Keep valuables secure and avoid displaying large amounts of cash. Be aware of your surroundings, especially in crowded areas. It's always a good idea to have a travel companion, especially when exploring less populated areas.
- Emergency Contacts: Know the local emergency contact numbers, including medical services, police, and your country's embassy or consulate.

By following these health and safety tips, you can ensure a safe and enjoyable trip to Gatlinburg, ready to handle any unexpected situations that might arise.

Travel Gadgets and Apps

Modern travel is made much easier and more enjoyable with the right gadgets and apps. Here are some essential travel gadgets and apps to consider for your trip to Gatlinburg:

Travel Gadgets:

- Smartphone: A smartphone is indispensable for navigation, photography, communication, and accessing travel information. Ensure it has a good camera, GPS capabilities, and sufficient storage for photos and videos.

- Portable Charger: A portable charger or power bank ensures your devices stay charged during long days of exploring. Choose one with multiple USB ports and a high capacity for convenience.
- Camera: While smartphones can take great photos, a dedicated camera with higher resolution and better zoom capabilities can enhance your photography experience, especially for capturing scenic landscapes and wildlife.
- Travel Adapter: If you're traveling internationally, a universal travel adapter is crucial to keep your devices powered. Look for one with multiple plug options and USB ports.
- Noise-Canceling Headphones: These are perfect for enjoying music or podcasts during your travels and can be especially helpful on flights or in noisy environments.
- Bluetooth Speaker: A compact Bluetooth speaker can enhance your travel experience

by allowing you to play your favorite music wherever you go.

- Reusable Water Bottle: Staying hydrated is essential, and a reusable water bottle with a built-in filter can ensure you have access to clean drinking water.

Travel Apps:

- Navigation Apps: Google Maps and Waze are essential for navigating unfamiliar areas. They provide real-time traffic updates, directions, and information about nearby attractions and services.
- Accommodation Apps: Apps like Airbnb, Booking.com, and Hotels.com help you find and book accommodations. They often offer reviews, photos, and competitive prices.
- Transportation Apps: Uber, Lyft, and local taxi apps can make getting around town convenient. For public transportation, the

Gatlinburg Trolley app provides schedules and route information.

- Weather Apps: Apps like AccuWeather or Weather.com provide up-to-date weather forecasts, helping you plan your activities accordingly.

- Travel Guides and Trip Planning Apps: TripAdvisor, Lonely Planet, and AllTrails offer comprehensive travel guides, reviews, and tips from other travelers. AllTrails is especially useful for finding and navigating hiking trails.

- Language Translation Apps: Google Translate can be handy if you encounter language barriers. It provides translations for text, speech, and even photos.

- Expense Tracking Apps: Splitwise and Trail Wallet help you keep track of your expenses, manage your budget, and share costs with travel companions.

- Emergency Apps: Apps like ICE (In Case of Emergency) store important medical information and emergency contacts, which can be accessed quickly in case of an emergency.

Utilizing these travel gadgets and apps will enhance your Gatlinburg experience, making it more convenient, enjoyable, and stress-free.

Chapter 5: Entry and Visa Requirements

Visa and Passport Information

Traveling to Gatlinburg, Tennessee, a popular tourist destination in the United States, requires careful attention to visa and passport requirements. Citizens of different countries may have varying entry needs depending on their nationality.

For most travelers, a valid passport is the primary requirement for entry into the United States. Ensure your passport is valid for at least six months beyond your intended stay. It is a good practice to have extra pages available for any potential visa stamps or entry stamps.

Visa Requirements:

- Visa Waiver Program (VWP): Citizens of VWP countries do not need a visa for stays of up to 90 days. Instead, they must apply for an Electronic System for Travel Authorization (ESTA) before traveling. This online application is quick, generally approved within minutes, and costs a nominal fee. Check the U.S. Department of Homeland Security's website to see if your country is part of the VWP.

- Non-VWP Countries: If your country is not part of the VWP, you must apply for a visa through the U.S. embassy or consulate in your home country. The most common type for tourists is the B-2 visa. The application involves filling out Form DS-160, paying a visa fee, and attending an interview where you'll need to provide proof of the purpose of your visit, financial stability, and ties to your home country.

Processing Times:

Visa processing times can vary, so it's crucial to apply well in advance of your planned travel date.

Standard processing time can range from a few weeks to several months. An expedited service is available for urgent situations but at a higher cost.

Additional Documents:

Regardless of your visa status, you may be required to show additional documents at the border. These might include proof of accommodation, return flight tickets, and evidence of sufficient funds to cover your stay.

Travel Restrictions and Updates:

Travel restrictions and requirements can change frequently. It's advisable to consult the U.S. Department of State's website or contact your local U.S. embassy for the latest updates on visa requirements and entry policies, especially if traveling during periods of heightened security or health concerns.

Customs Regulations

Upon arrival in Gatlinburg, visitors must adhere to U.S. customs regulations. These rules govern what you can bring into the country and ensure compliance with local laws.

Prohibited Items

Certain items are strictly prohibited from entry into the U.S. These include illegal drugs, certain agricultural products, and weapons. Bringing in items such as fresh fruits, vegetables, or meats is restricted to prevent the spread of pests and diseases. For specific items, check with U.S. Customs and Border Protection (CBP) guidelines before departure.

Duty-Free Allowances

Travelers are allowed to bring in a limited amount of goods duty-free. For instance, you can bring up to $800 worth of merchandise into the U.S. duty-free. This amount includes items purchased abroad, gifts, and personal goods. If you exceed this allowance, you must declare the excess goods and pay the appropriate duties and taxes.

Declaring Items

When arriving in the U.S., you must declare all items that exceed your personal exemption or that you are unsure about. The CBP declaration form, usually provided during your flight, requires you to list these items. Failure to declare can result in fines or confiscation of goods.

Currency and Financial Regulations

There is no limit to the amount of U.S. dollars you can bring into the country, but if you're carrying more than $10,000 in currency or monetary instruments, you must declare it to CBP. This includes traveler's checks, money orders, and negotiable instruments.

Customs Procedures

Upon arrival, you will go through customs where officers may ask questions about your travel plans and inspect your belongings. It's important to answer all questions truthfully and comply with any inspection requests to avoid complications.

Travel Insurance Requirements

Travel insurance is highly recommended for anyone traveling to Gatlinburg. It provides essential protection against unexpected events that could impact your trip.

Types of Coverage:

- Medical Insurance: Covers expenses related to medical emergencies during your trip, including hospital stays, doctor visits, and prescription medications. U.S. healthcare can be expensive, and having medical insurance ensures you are protected from high costs if you need treatment.

- Trip Cancellation and Interruption: Provides reimbursement for non-refundable expenses if you need to cancel or cut short your trip due to unforeseen circumstances like illness, family emergencies, or natural disasters.

- Lost or Delayed Baggage: Covers the cost of replacing lost or delayed luggage, including personal items and essential necessities.

- Travel Delays: Compensation for expenses incurred due to delays in your flight or other travel arrangements, such as accommodation and food costs.

Choosing a Policy:

When selecting a travel insurance policy, consider factors such as coverage limits, exclusions, and the provider's reputation. Some policies offer comprehensive packages that cover a wide range of scenarios, while others may be more basic.

Purchasing Insurance:

Travel insurance can be purchased through travel agencies, insurance companies, or online comparison tools. It is advisable to compare different plans to find one that fits your needs and budget.

Making Claims:

If you need to make a claim, contact your insurance provider as soon as possible. Keep detailed records and receipts of any expenses related to your claim. Adhering to the policy's claim process will help ensure a smooth and successful reimbursement.

By understanding these entry and visa requirements, customs regulations, and travel insurance needs, you can prepare effectively for your trip to Gatlinburg, ensuring a smooth and enjoyable experience.

Chapter 6: Itinerary

Overview of Activities

Gatlinburg, nestled in the heart of the Great Smoky Mountains, offers a rich array of activities that cater to various interests, from nature enthusiasts to thrill-seekers and culture buffs. Crafting a well-rounded itinerary can help you make the most of your visit and ensure you experience the best this charming town has to offer.

Outdoor Adventures

Gatlinburg is renowned for its proximity to the Great Smoky Mountains National Park, which offers a plethora of outdoor activities. Hiking is a must-do, with trails ranging from easy walks to challenging climbs. Popular trails include the Alum Cave Trail, which leads to a stunning viewpoint, and the Laurel Falls Trail, known for its picturesque waterfall. For those who enjoy a scenic drive, the

Cades Cove Loop Road provides breathtaking views of the park's wildlife and historic structures.

In addition to hiking, the park offers opportunities for wildlife viewing, picnicking, and camping. Fishing enthusiasts can enjoy fly-fishing in the park's streams, while those seeking more adventure can try horseback riding along the park's equestrian trails.

Family-Friendly Activities

Gatlinburg is a family-friendly destination with numerous attractions that appeal to all ages. The Ripley's Aquarium of the Smokies is a highlight, featuring a variety of marine life, including sharks, rays, and colorful fish. The aquarium's underwater tunnel provides a unique view of marine animals swimming overhead.

For a mix of fun and education, visit the Gatlinburg Space Needle, where you can enjoy panoramic views of the Smokies from the observation deck.

The nearby Ober Gatlinburg offers a range of activities, including an amusement park, ice skating rink, and a scenic tramway.

Cultural and Historical Sites

Explore Gatlinburg's rich heritage by visiting sites such as the Great Smoky Mountains Heritage Center, which showcases the region's history through exhibits and artifacts. The city's arts and crafts community is another cultural gem, with numerous galleries and shops featuring handmade crafts, paintings, and sculptures.

Don't miss the chance to experience a traditional Southern meal at one of Gatlinburg's renowned restaurants, where you can savor local specialties like biscuits and gravy, fried chicken, and apple pie.

Shopping and Entertainment

Gatlinburg boasts a vibrant shopping scene, with numerous shops offering everything from unique souvenirs to local art. The Gatlinburg Strip, a bustling area in the heart of the city, is lined with shops, boutiques, and attractions.

Evening entertainment is abundant, with options ranging from live music and comedy shows to thrilling rides and games at local amusement centers. The variety of entertainment options ensures that there's something for everyone to enjoy after a day of exploring.

Day-by-Day Breakdown

Day 1: Arrival and Exploration

- Morning: Arrive in Gatlinburg and check into your accommodation. Take some time to settle in and get familiar with your surroundings. If you're staying in a cabin or lodge, enjoy the scenic views and relax after your journey.
- Afternoon: Start your exploration with a visit to the Great Smoky Mountains National

Park. Take a short, easy hike on the Laurel Falls Trail to acclimate yourself and enjoy the beauty of the park.

- Evening: Head to downtown Gatlinburg for a leisurely stroll along the Gatlinburg Strip. Browse local shops and pick up any essentials or souvenirs. Enjoy dinner at a local restaurant, trying some Southern comfort food.

Day 2: Outdoor Adventure and Family Fun

- Morning: Begin the day with a more challenging hike, such as the Alum Cave Trail, which offers stunning views and a rewarding experience. Pack a picnic lunch to enjoy at one of the park's designated areas.
- Afternoon: After your hike, visit the Ripley's Aquarium of the Smokies for an afternoon of family-friendly fun. Explore the various exhibits and interactive displays.

- Evening: Take a ride on the Gatlinburg SkyLift or visit the Gatlinburg Space Needle for panoramic views of the city and surrounding mountains. Enjoy dinner at a different local restaurant or explore the culinary scene further.

Day 3: Cultural Exploration and Relaxation

- Morning: Visit the Great Smoky Mountains Heritage Center to learn more about the region's history and culture. Explore the exhibits and take a guided tour if available.
- Afternoon: Spend some time exploring the arts and crafts community. Visit local galleries and shops to view and purchase handmade crafts, paintings, and other unique items.
- Evening: Enjoy a relaxing evening at one of Gatlinburg's entertainment venues, such as a live music show or a comedy performance. Alternatively, visit Ober Gatlinburg for some

evening fun, including ice skating or a tram ride.

Day 4: Scenic Drives and Departure

- Morning: Take a scenic drive through the Smokies, such as the Cades Cove Loop Road, which offers beautiful vistas and opportunities to spot wildlife. Stop at historic sites along the way to learn more about the area's history.
- Afternoon: Return to Gatlinburg and take some time to explore any remaining attractions or shops you might have missed. Enjoy a final meal at one of your favorite restaurants.
- Evening: Check out of your accommodation and prepare for your departure. Reflect on your trip and plan your next visit to this charming mountain town.

Tips for a Flexible Itinerary

Creating a flexible itinerary is key to making the most of your trip to Gatlinburg. While having a plan is essential, being adaptable ensures that you can enjoy your vacation without stress.

Prioritize Key Activities

Identify your must-see attractions and activities, and plan to visit them early in your trip. This ensures that you experience your top priorities even if other plans change. For example, if hiking is a top priority, make sure to schedule time for it and have alternative options in case of bad weather.

Allow for Downtime

Incorporate some free time into your itinerary. This allows you to relax, explore unexpected discoveries, or adjust plans based on how you're feeling. Downtime can be spent leisurely walking around town, enjoying a coffee at a local café, or simply taking in the views.

Be Prepared for Weather Changes

The weather in the Smoky Mountains can be unpredictable. Have backup plans for indoor activities in case of rain or other unfavorable conditions. For instance, if hiking is not feasible due to weather, you could visit a museum or enjoy a movie at a local theater.

Use Local Recommendations

Talk to locals or your accommodation staff for recommendations on activities or places to visit. Locals often know about hidden gems or current events that might not be in your guidebook. Their suggestions can help you discover new experiences and adjust your itinerary accordingly.

Stay Flexible with Meal Plans

While it's helpful to have a list of recommended restaurants, be open to trying new places that you come across during your travels. Sometimes the best dining experiences are found spontaneously. If you have specific dietary needs, research restaurants in advance but remain flexible to accommodate any changes.

Manage Time Wisely
Avoid overloading your schedule with too many activities. Allow enough time for each activity and include some buffer time between them. This prevents the stress of rushing and ensures that you can fully enjoy each experience.

Keep Essentials Handy
Always have essentials such as a map, weather app, and contact information for your accommodation. Having these resources readily available can help you make quick decisions and navigate any changes to your plans.

Embrace Spontaneity
Sometimes the best travel experiences come from spontaneous adventures. Be open to adjusting your plans based on new opportunities, whether it's

joining a local festival, exploring an unexpected attraction, or simply taking a detour to enjoy a scenic spot.

By incorporating these tips into your travel plans, you can create a flexible and enjoyable itinerary that allows you to fully experience the diverse offerings of Gatlinburg while adapting to any changes or surprises that come your way.

Chapter 7: Hotels and Accommodations

Choosing the Right Area to Stay

When planning your trip to Gatlinburg, selecting the right area to stay can greatly enhance your overall experience. Gatlinburg offers various lodging options, each catering to different preferences and needs. Here's a guide to help you choose the best area for your stay.

Downtown Gatlinburg

Staying in downtown Gatlinburg places you in the heart of the action. This area is ideal if you want to be close to restaurants, shops, and entertainment options. The Gatlinburg Strip, a bustling area filled with attractions like the Gatlinburg SkyLift, Ripley's Aquarium of the Smokies, and a variety of dining options, is within walking distance from many hotels and motels. Being centrally located means you can easily explore local shops and cafes, making it a convenient choice for those who prefer to walk to attractions.

Near the Great Smoky Mountains National Park

If you're visiting Gatlinburg primarily for outdoor activities and natural beauty, consider staying closer to the entrance of the Great Smoky Mountains National Park. Lodging options in this area often include cabins, lodges, and campgrounds that offer quick access to hiking trails, scenic drives, and wildlife viewing. Staying here provides a more serene experience, with the added benefit of being immersed in nature. Some accommodations may offer spectacular views of the mountains and immediate access to park activities.

Riverfront Accommodations

The Little Pigeon River runs through Gatlinburg, and staying in a riverfront accommodation can provide a relaxing and scenic experience. Many hotels, motels, and cabin rentals along the river offer picturesque views and the soothing sound of flowing water. Riverfront locations are often quieter than downtown, making them a great choice for visitors looking to enjoy both nature and convenience. Some riverfront properties even feature private balconies or patios where you can unwind while enjoying the view.

Outskirts and Suburban Areas

For those who prefer a more tranquil setting away from the bustling tourist areas, the outskirts and suburban areas of Gatlinburg offer a peaceful retreat. These locations might be a short drive from downtown but provide a quieter environment with larger properties and more space. If you're traveling with a family or a group, renting a cabin or a larger home in these areas can offer more privacy and amenities, such as fully equipped kitchens and private yards.

Proximity to Attractions

Consider the proximity of your accommodation to specific attractions you plan to visit. For example, if you're interested in visiting the Ober Gatlinburg amusement park or taking scenic tram rides, staying in the vicinity can save you time and transportation costs. Similarly, if you have specific interests, like visiting the Smoky Mountain Alpine Coaster or the Gatlinburg Arts and Crafts Community, choose a location that minimizes travel time to these spots.

Accessibility and Transportation

Evaluate the accessibility of your chosen area, especially if you're traveling without a car. Some areas in Gatlinburg are more walkable, while others might require a vehicle or public transportation. Downtown Gatlinburg offers easy access to trolley services and is pedestrian-friendly, whereas more remote accommodations might necessitate driving to reach various attractions and amenities.

Luxury Hotels

For those seeking an upscale experience, Gatlinburg offers several luxury hotels that provide exceptional service, amenities, and comfort. These establishments are perfect for travelers looking to indulge in a high-end vacation.

The Park Vista – a DoubleTree by Hilton Hotel

The Park Vista is a premier luxury hotel located in the heart of Gatlinburg, offering stunning panoramic views of the Great Smoky Mountains. This hotel boasts a range of luxurious amenities, including spacious rooms and suites with contemporary décor, an indoor pool, a fitness center, and a full-service restaurant. The hotel's signature feature is its 15-story atrium, which provides a breathtaking backdrop and a relaxing environment for guests.

Margaritaville Resort Gatlinburg

Inspired by the laid-back lifestyle of Jimmy Buffett, Margaritaville Resort Gatlinburg combines luxury with a fun, tropical ambiance. The resort features upscale rooms and suites with modern décor and private balconies. Guests can enjoy a range of amenities, including a spa, an outdoor pool with a lazy river, a fitness center, and a variety of dining options. The resort's unique atmosphere and proximity to downtown attractions make it a popular choice for those seeking both luxury and entertainment.

The Lodge at Buckberry Creek

Situated on a secluded hillside, The Lodge at Buckberry Creek offers a luxurious and serene retreat with stunning views of the Smoky Mountains. The lodge features elegant rooms and suites with rustic, yet refined décor, and a range of high-end amenities, including a full-service restaurant, a spa, and an outdoor pool. Its secluded location provides a peaceful escape while still being within a short drive of Gatlinburg's attractions.

Anakeesta Treehouse Village

For a unique luxury experience, consider staying at Anakeesta's Treehouse Village. Located in the Anakeesta Adventure Park, these treehouses offer a blend of luxury and adventure, with stunning views of the surrounding forest and mountains. Each treehouse is equipped with upscale amenities, and guests have access to exclusive park experiences, including zip-lining and treetop walks.

The Gatlinburg Cabin Rentals

Several luxury cabin rental options are available for those seeking a more private and personalized experience. These cabins often feature high-end furnishings, gourmet kitchens, and private hot tubs or pools. Many are located in picturesque settings with panoramic mountain views, providing a perfect blend of luxury and nature.

The Details

Luxury hotels in Gatlinburg often include additional perks such as concierge services, valet parking, and exclusive access to amenities. These details enhance the overall experience and ensure that your stay is as comfortable and enjoyable as possible.

Budget-Friendly Hotels

Traveling to Gatlinburg doesn't mean you have to compromise on comfort and quality if you're on a budget. The area offers a range of affordable accommodation options that provide value for money without sacrificing essential amenities.

Quality Inn & Suites Gatlinburg

Quality Inn & Suites offers a comfortable and budget-friendly stay in Gatlinburg. Located within a short distance of downtown attractions, this hotel features spacious rooms with basic amenities such as free Wi-Fi, complimentary breakfast, and an indoor pool. It's an excellent choice for travelers looking for convenience and affordability.

Baymont by Wyndham Gatlinburg On The River

Baymont by Wyndham provides a budget-friendly option with a picturesque location along the Little Pigeon River. The hotel offers comfortable rooms with essential amenities, including free breakfast, Wi-Fi, and an outdoor pool. Its proximity to downtown Gatlinburg and the peaceful riverfront setting make it a popular choice for economical travelers.

Sleep Inn & Suites

Sleep Inn & Suites is another affordable option that offers a pleasant stay without breaking the bank. The hotel features clean and comfortable rooms with modern amenities, including free breakfast, Wi-Fi, and an indoor pool. Its location provides easy access to local attractions and shopping areas.

Econo Lodge Inn & Suites

Econo Lodge Inn & Suites offers basic accommodations at a budget-friendly price. The hotel features standard rooms with essential amenities, including free Wi-Fi, breakfast, and parking. Its location provides convenient access to Gatlinburg's attractions and is a good choice for travelers looking for economical lodging.

Days Inn by Wyndham Gatlinburg on the River

Days Inn offers affordable lodging with a focus on value. Located near the river, the hotel features rooms with standard amenities such as free Wi-Fi, breakfast, and an outdoor pool. The proximity to both natural attractions and downtown Gatlinburg makes it a practical choice for budget-conscious travelers.

Tips for Finding Budget Accommodations

Book in Advance: To secure the best rates, book your accommodations well in advance, especially during peak seasons.

- Look for Deals and Discounts: Check for special promotions, discounts, and package deals that can offer additional savings.
- Consider Alternative Lodging: Look into vacation rentals, motels, and hostels as alternative budget-friendly options.
- Read Reviews: Before booking, read guest reviews to ensure that the hotel meets your expectations in terms of cleanliness, service, and overall quality.

By understanding the different areas and types of accommodations available in Gatlinburg, you can choose the lodging that best fits your preferences and budget, ensuring a comfortable and enjoyable stay.

Chapter 8: Tourist Centers and Locations

Must-See Attractions

Gatlinburg is packed with attractions that cater to a wide range of interests. Here are some must-see highlights that should be on every visitor's itinerary:

Ripley's Aquarium of the Smokies

One of Gatlinburg's most popular attractions, Ripley's Aquarium of the Smokies offers an immersive experience into the world of marine life. The aquarium features an extensive collection of aquatic species, including sharks, rays, and exotic fish. Highlights include the Shark Tunnel, where visitors can walk through a glass tunnel surrounded by swimming sharks and rays, and the Penguin Playhouse, home to a lively colony of penguins.

Ober Gatlinburg

Ober Gatlinburg is a year-round amusement park and ski resort located just a short drive from downtown. In winter, it offers skiing, snowboarding, and ice skating, while summer visitors can enjoy a range of activities including a scenic tram ride, alpine slides, and an observation tower with panoramic views. The resort also features a wildlife encounter area with bears, otters, and other native species.

Gatlinburg SkyLift

For breathtaking views of the Smoky Mountains, the Gatlinburg SkyLift is a must-visit. This iconic chairlift takes visitors up to the top of Crockett Mountain, providing panoramic views of Gatlinburg and the surrounding landscape. The recently expanded SkyLift Park includes a SkyDeck and SkyBridge, the longest pedestrian suspension bridge in North America, offering stunning vistas and a thrilling walking experience.

The Great Smoky Mountains National Park

As America's most visited national park, the Great Smoky Mountains National Park is a natural wonder that attracts millions of visitors annually. Key attractions within the park include Clingmans Dome, the highest point in Tennessee, which offers a panoramic observation tower with 360-degree views. Other popular spots are Cades Cove, a picturesque valley with historic structures and abundant wildlife, and the picturesque Laurel Falls, known for its beautiful waterfall.

Anakeesta

Anakeesta is a family-friendly adventure park that combines natural beauty with fun attractions. Visitors can explore the Treehouse Village, walk across the treetop canopy in the Chondola, and enjoy interactive exhibits. The park also features a stunning mountain garden, shopping, and dining options, making it a comprehensive destination for outdoor and family entertainment.

Off-the-Beaten-Path Spots

For those looking to explore less crowded and unique spots in Gatlinburg, here are some off-the-beaten-path destinations:

Roaring Fork Motor Nature Trail

A lesser-known gem, the Roaring Fork Motor Nature Trail is a scenic loop road that offers a more tranquil experience compared to the park's more popular spots. The trail winds through lush forest and historic log cabins, with opportunities for wildlife viewing and serene walks. Highlights include the Noah "Bud" Ogle Cabin and the remnants of old homesteads.

The Arts and Crafts Community

The Great Smoky Arts and Crafts Community, located just a short drive from downtown Gatlinburg, is a hidden treasure for those interested in local art and crafts. This 8-mile loop features over 100 artisans showcasing handmade goods, from pottery and woodworking to textiles and paintings. Visitors can explore galleries, workshops, and shops, gaining insight into the region's artistic traditions.

The Salt and Pepper Shaker Museum

A quirky and charming destination, the Salt and Pepper Shaker Museum houses an extensive collection of over 20,000 salt and pepper shakers from around the world. The museum, which is one of the largest of its kind, offers a whimsical look at this everyday kitchen item through various historical and thematic displays.

The Old Mill Square

Located just a short drive from Gatlinburg, the Old Mill Square in Pigeon Forge offers a glimpse into the past with its historic mill, charming shops, and eateries. The area features the Old Mill, a functioning gristmill that has been in operation since 1830, and offers freshly ground cornmeal and other products. Visitors can explore the quaint shops and enjoy Southern-style meals at the Old Mill Restaurant.

The Gatlinburg Bypass

The Gatlinburg Bypass is a scenic drive that provides a quieter alternative to the main routes into the city. The bypass offers picturesque views of the surrounding mountains and valleys and allows for a more relaxed approach to entering Gatlinburg. It's an excellent route for those looking to escape the hustle and bustle of the main tourist areas.

Nature and Outdoor Activities

Gatlinburg is renowned for its access to outdoor adventures and natural beauty. Here are some top activities for nature lovers and outdoor enthusiasts:

Hiking Trails

The Great Smoky Mountains National Park is a hiker's paradise, with over 800 miles of trails ranging from easy walks to challenging backcountry routes. Popular trails include the Alum Cave Trail, which leads to a dramatic overlook with sweeping views, and the Chimney Tops Trail, known for its strenuous climb and rewarding vistas at the summit. The park's trails offer opportunities to experience diverse ecosystems, including dense forests, waterfalls, and high mountain ridges.

Fishing and Water Activities

The park's numerous streams and rivers provide excellent fishing opportunities. The streams are stocked with trout, making them ideal for fly-fishing enthusiasts. Popular fishing spots include the streams in Elkmont and the middle prong of the Little Pigeon River. Additionally, kayaking and canoeing are enjoyable activities on the park's larger bodies of water, such as the Fontana Lake and the Lake Arrowhead area.

Scenic Drives

For those who prefer a more leisurely way to enjoy the natural beauty of the Smokies, scenic drives offer spectacular views without the physical exertion of hiking. The Newfound Gap Road provides a stunning cross-section of the park, offering scenic overlooks and opportunities to stop and take in the views. The Foothills Parkway, another scenic route, offers panoramic vistas of the park and surrounding landscapes.

Camping

Camping is a fantastic way to immerse yourself in the natural beauty of Gatlinburg. The Great Smoky Mountains National Park offers several campgrounds, including Elkmont, Smokemont, and Cosby. Each campground provides access to the park's trails and natural attractions, and reservations are recommended, especially during peak seasons. For a more rustic experience, backcountry camping is available for those who seek solitude and a deeper connection with nature.

Wildlife Viewing

Gatlinburg is a prime location for wildlife viewing. The Great Smoky Mountains National Park is home to a diverse range of animals, including black bears, deer, and wild turkeys. Cades Cove, a picturesque valley within the park, is particularly renowned for its wildlife sightings. Early mornings and late afternoons are the best times to spot animals as they are more active during these times.

These activities offer a comprehensive view of Gatlinburg's natural beauty and provide various ways to enjoy the outdoors, whether through adventurous pursuits or peaceful observations.

Chapter 9: Cultural Experiences

Local Festivals and Events

Gatlinburg, with its vibrant community and picturesque setting, hosts a variety of local festivals and events throughout the year that showcase the region's culture and charm. These celebrations offer visitors a chance to experience local traditions, cuisine, and entertainment.

Gatlinburg Winter Magic

Starting in early November and running through February, Gatlinburg Winter Magic transforms the city into a winter wonderland. The festival features millions of lights that illuminate the streets, creating a festive atmosphere. Visitors can enjoy light displays, holiday-themed events, and seasonal decorations. Winter Magic is an excellent way to experience Gatlinburg's holiday spirit and enjoy the town's charming winter scenery.

Smoky Mountain Harvest Festival

Held from mid-September through October, the Smoky Mountain Harvest Festival celebrates the fall season with a variety of events and activities. The festival includes a cornucopia of harvest-themed events such as farmers' markets, craft fairs, and pumpkin patches. Visitors can explore local produce, handmade crafts, and enjoy traditional fall foods. This festival offers a wonderful way to experience the local agricultural heritage and autumnal beauty of the region.

Gatlinburg Craftsmen's Fair

The Gatlinburg Craftsmen's Fair takes place twice a year—during the summer and fall—and features over 200 craftsmen showcasing their handmade goods. The fair includes a wide array of crafts, including pottery, jewelry, woodworking, and textiles. Attendees can interact with artisans, watch live demonstrations, and purchase unique handcrafted items. The fair highlights Gatlinburg's strong tradition of arts and crafts and provides visitors with a chance to support local artists.

Fourth of July Parade and Fireworks

The Fourth of July celebrations in Gatlinburg are renowned for their small-town charm and festive atmosphere. The annual parade kicks off with colorful floats, marching bands, and patriotic displays. In the evening, the skies above Gatlinburg light up with a spectacular fireworks show, which is one of the largest in the region. This celebration is a great way to experience the community spirit and festive atmosphere of Gatlinburg during Independence Day.

Smoky Mountain Songwriters Festival

Held annually in August, the Smoky Mountain Songwriters Festival brings together aspiring and established songwriters for a series of performances and workshops. The festival includes live music events, songwriter showcases, and educational sessions. It provides an opportunity to experience a diverse range of musical styles and support local and regional talent.

Museums and Historical Sites

Gatlinburg and the surrounding area offer a range of museums and historical sites that provide insight into the region's rich heritage and culture.

Great Smoky Mountains Heritage Center

Located in nearby Townsend, the Great Smoky Mountains Heritage Center offers a comprehensive look at the history and culture of the Smoky Mountains region. The center features exhibits on Appalachian life, including artifacts, photographs, and interactive displays. Visitors can learn about the area's Native American heritage, early settlers, and the impact of the Great Smoky Mountains National Park on the local community.

The Old Mill

The Old Mill, situated in Pigeon Forge, is a historic gristmill that dates back to the 1830s. The mill is still in operation today, producing cornmeal, flour, and other products using traditional methods. Visitors can tour the mill, learn about its history, and purchase freshly ground products. The Old Mill area also includes a restaurant and shops that offer Southern-style meals and handmade goods.

Gatlinburg Trolley Tour of Lights

For a unique historical experience, consider taking the Gatlinburg Trolley Tour of Lights during the holiday season. This tour provides a guided overview of Gatlinburg's history and significant landmarks, all while showcasing the town's festive light displays. It's a relaxing way to learn about Gatlinburg's past while enjoying the holiday decorations.

Mountain Farm Museum

Located within the Great Smoky Mountains National Park, the Mountain Farm Museum is an open-air museum that features historic log structures and farm equipment. The museum provides a glimpse into the daily life of early Appalachian settlers, showcasing preserved buildings such as a blacksmith shop, a barn, and a farmhouse. It offers educational programs and demonstrations that highlight traditional farming practices and rural life.

The Heritage Museum

Situated in nearby Sevierville, the Heritage Museum focuses on the history and culture of the Sevier County area. The museum features exhibits on local history, including early pioneer life, the development of the region, and notable historical figures. It offers a comprehensive look at the area's past and provides context for understanding the broader history of the Smoky Mountain region.

Art and Music Scene

Gatlinburg's art and music scene reflects the area's creative spirit and provides numerous opportunities for cultural enrichment.

Gatlinburg Arts and Crafts Community

The Gatlinburg Arts and Crafts Community is an 8-mile loop featuring over 100 artisans who create and sell handmade crafts. This community includes studios, galleries, and shops where visitors can view and purchase unique artworks, including pottery, woodworking, painting, and textiles. The community is a testament to Gatlinburg's vibrant arts scene and offers an opportunity to meet local artists and purchase one-of-a-kind items.

The Smoky Mountain Tunes and Tales

Smoky Mountain Tunes and Tales is an annual summer event that takes place in downtown Gatlinburg. The event features live performances by musicians, storytellers, and costumed characters who bring Appalachian folk tales and traditional music to life. Performers can be found throughout the streets, creating a lively and immersive cultural experience for visitors.

Gatlinburg Gallery

The Gatlinburg Gallery is a local art gallery that showcases a range of artwork from regional artists. The gallery features rotating exhibits, including paintings, photography, and sculptures. It provides a platform for local artists to display their work and offers visitors the chance to explore contemporary and traditional art forms.

The Sevier County Fair

Held annually in nearby Sevierville, the Sevier County Fair includes a variety of musical performances, art exhibits, and cultural activities. The fair features local musicians, including bluegrass bands and country artists, as well as craft and art vendors. It's a great way to experience the local music scene and explore regional artistic talents.

Live Music Venues

Gatlinburg and the surrounding areas host several live music venues that offer performances by local and regional artists. Venues such as the Smoky Mountain Opry and the Island in Pigeon Forge provide a range of musical styles, from country and bluegrass to gospel and rock. These venues offer a lively atmosphere and showcase the diverse musical heritage of the Smoky Mountains.

Gatlinburg's cultural experiences encompass a rich tapestry of local festivals, historical sites, and vibrant art and music scenes, providing visitors with a well-rounded understanding of the region's heritage and creative spirit.

Chapter 10: Luxury Hotels

The Park Vista – a DoubleTree by Hilton Hotel

The Park Vista – a DoubleTree by Hilton Hotel stands out as one of Gatlinburg's premier luxury accommodations. Perched on a hilltop with sweeping views of the Great Smoky Mountains, this 15-story hotel offers both stunning vistas and an array of upscale amenities that cater to a diverse range of travelers.

Accommodations

The Park Vista features 300 guest rooms and suites that are designed with modern elegance and comfort in mind. Each room boasts contemporary décor with neutral tones and stylish furnishings. Guests can enjoy a range of accommodations, from standard rooms with panoramic mountain views to expansive suites with separate living areas and upgraded amenities. All rooms include luxurious bedding, high-speed Wi-Fi, flat-screen TVs, and mini-fridges.

Amenities

The hotel's amenities are designed to enhance the guest experience. One of the standout features is the 15-story atrium, which creates a dramatic and inviting atmosphere. The indoor pool, with its cascading waterfall and scenic views, is a popular spot for relaxation. The hotel also offers a well-equipped fitness center, a full-service restaurant, and a lobby bar. For those seeking relaxation, the Park Vista provides a spacious outdoor terrace with seating areas, ideal for enjoying the mountain views.

Dining

The hotel's on-site restaurant, Vista Grill, serves a variety of American cuisine with a focus on fresh, local ingredients. Guests can enjoy breakfast, lunch, and dinner while taking in views of the surrounding mountains. The Vista Lounge offers a more casual dining experience and a selection of cocktails and light fare. Room service is also available for those who prefer to dine in the comfort of their room.

Location

The Park Vista is conveniently located near the heart of Gatlinburg, providing easy access to local attractions such as the Gatlinburg SkyLift, Ripley's Aquarium, and the Great Smoky Mountains National Park. The hotel's elevated position offers a tranquil retreat from the hustle and bustle of downtown while remaining close to popular sights and activities.

Services

The hotel offers a range of services to ensure a comfortable stay. These include a 24-hour front desk, concierge services, valet parking, and business center facilities. The Park Vista is also a popular choice for events and meetings, with versatile event spaces and dedicated event planning services.

Margaritaville Resort Gatlinburg

Inspired by the laid-back lifestyle of Jimmy Buffett, Margaritaville Resort Gatlinburg brings a touch of tropical paradise to the Smoky Mountains. This resort combines luxury with a fun, casual atmosphere, making it a favorite among families and couples alike.

Accommodations

The Margaritaville Resort Gatlinburg features a variety of room types, including standard rooms, suites, and even private cottages. Each room is designed with a vibrant, tropical theme that reflects the resort's relaxed ambiance. Guests can enjoy comfortable bedding, flat-screen TVs, mini-fridges, and private balconies or patios with views of the surrounding mountains or the resort's amenities.

Amenities

The resort offers a range of amenities designed to provide a fun and relaxing experience. The outdoor pool area is a highlight, featuring a lazy river, water slides, and cabanas for rent. The resort also boasts a full-service spa, a fitness center, and a game room. For dining, visitors can choose from several on-site options, including the Margaritaville Restaurant, which serves a variety of tropical dishes and cocktails in a lively setting.

Dining

Margaritaville Resort Gatlinburg offers a diverse dining experience. The Margaritaville Restaurant is a popular choice, featuring a menu of island-inspired cuisine and a laid-back atmosphere. The restaurant's décor and music create a festive environment, reflecting the resort's tropical theme. Additionally, the resort has a coffee shop and a poolside bar, providing convenient options for casual dining and refreshments.

Location

Situated within walking distance of downtown Gatlinburg, the Margaritaville Resort provides easy access to local attractions such as the Gatlinburg SkyLift, Ripley's Aquarium, and the Great Smoky Mountains National Park. The resort's central location allows guests to explore the area while enjoying the resort's unique amenities.

Services

The resort offers a range of services to enhance the guest experience, including concierge assistance, a 24-hour front desk, and valet parking. The Margaritaville Resort is also a popular venue for weddings and special events, with dedicated event planning services and versatile event spaces.

The Lodge at Buckberry Creek

The Lodge at Buckberry Creek offers a luxurious and secluded retreat in the Smoky Mountains, combining rustic charm with high-end amenities.

Located on a hillside with breathtaking views of the surrounding mountains, this lodge provides a tranquil escape with a focus on natural beauty and elegant comfort.

Accommodations

The Lodge at Buckberry Creek features a variety of accommodations, including lodge rooms, suites, and private cabins. Each room is designed with a blend of rustic and modern décor, featuring high-quality furnishings, stone fireplaces, and private balconies. The suites offer additional space and upscale amenities, such as jetted tubs and separate living areas. The lodge's cabins provide a more private and intimate experience, with fully equipped kitchens and stunning mountain views.

Amenities

The lodge's amenities are designed to provide a luxurious and relaxing experience. Guests can enjoy the on-site restaurant, which serves gourmet meals made from locally sourced ingredients. The lodge also features a full-service spa, an outdoor heated pool, and a fitness center. The property's expansive grounds include walking trails, gardens, and outdoor seating areas, allowing guests to immerse themselves in the natural beauty of the Smoky Mountains.

Dining

The Lodge at Buckberry Creek's restaurant offers a fine dining experience with a focus on regional cuisine. The menu features seasonal dishes prepared with fresh, local ingredients, and the restaurant's elegant setting provides a refined dining atmosphere. Guests can also enjoy outdoor dining on the restaurant's terrace, with picturesque views of the surrounding landscape.

Location

Situated on a private hillside, The Lodge at Buckberry Creek provides a secluded and serene environment while remaining within a short drive of Gatlinburg's attractions. The lodge's location offers easy access to the Great Smoky Mountains National Park, as well as nearby hiking trails and scenic viewpoints.

Services

The Lodge at Buckberry Creek offers a range of services to ensure a comfortable stay, including concierge assistance, a 24-hour front desk, and valet parking. The lodge is also a popular venue for weddings and special events, with dedicated event planning services and beautiful indoor and outdoor event spaces.

Each of these luxury hotels in Gatlinburg offers a unique experience, combining upscale amenities with stunning surroundings and exceptional service, ensuring a memorable stay for all guests.

Chapter 11: Budget-Friendly Hotels

Quality Inn & Suites Gatlinburg

Quality Inn & Suites Gatlinburg is an excellent choice for budget-conscious travelers seeking comfort and convenience in a prime location. Situated within easy reach of downtown Gatlinburg, this hotel provides a blend of affordability and practical amenities.

Accommodations

The hotel offers a variety of room types, including standard rooms and suites, catering to both solo travelers and families. Each room is equipped with essential amenities such as comfortable bedding, flat-screen TVs, mini-fridges, and free Wi-Fi. The rooms are designed to be cozy and functional, ensuring a pleasant stay without compromising on comfort.

Amenities

Quality Inn & Suites features a range of amenities designed to enhance the guest experience. The hotel provides a complimentary hot breakfast each morning, which includes a selection of hot and cold items to start the day off right. Other amenities include a seasonal outdoor pool, a fitness center, and free parking. For added convenience, the hotel has a 24-hour front desk and offers laundry facilities.

Location

Located just a short drive from the heart of Gatlinburg, Quality Inn & Suites offers easy access to popular attractions such as the Gatlinburg SkyLift and Ripley's Aquarium. The hotel's proximity to the city center makes it a convenient base for exploring the area while staying within a budget.

Services

The hotel's services are designed to provide value and convenience for guests. In addition to the standard amenities, Quality Inn & Suites offers business services, including a meeting room and fax/photocopying facilities. The friendly staff is available to assist with any inquiries or needs during the stay.

Baymont by Wyndham Gatlinburg On The River

Baymont by Wyndham Gatlinburg On The River offers a comfortable and affordable lodging option with a picturesque setting along the Little Pigeon River. This hotel provides a budget-friendly stay with a focus on convenience and a relaxing atmosphere.

Accommodations
Baymont by Wyndham features a range of room options, including standard rooms and suites, all

designed to be inviting and functional. Rooms come equipped with essential amenities such as free Wi-Fi, flat-screen TVs, mini-fridges, and microwaves. The decor is simple yet comfortable, ensuring a pleasant stay for all guests.

Amenities

The hotel offers several amenities aimed at enhancing guest comfort. A complimentary continental breakfast is served each morning, providing a variety of options to start the day. The hotel also features an outdoor pool, which is perfect for unwinding after a day of exploring. Other amenities include a fitness center, a business center, and free parking. The hotel's riverside setting provides a tranquil backdrop for relaxation.

Location

Baymont by Wyndham is conveniently located near downtown Gatlinburg, offering easy access to popular attractions such as the Great Smoky Mountains National Park and Gatlinburg SkyLift.

The hotel's riverside location also provides a serene environment, adding to the overall appeal of the stay.

Services

The hotel offers practical services to ensure a hassle-free stay, including a 24-hour front desk, laundry facilities, and business services. The staff is known for being accommodating and helpful, providing a welcoming atmosphere for guests.

Sleep Inn & Suites

Sleep Inn & Suites provides a budget-friendly yet comfortable lodging option in Gatlinburg, focusing on affordability without sacrificing quality. This hotel is ideal for travelers seeking a convenient and cost-effective stay while enjoying modern amenities.

Accommodations

Sleep Inn & Suites offers a range of room types, including standard rooms and suites, designed for comfort and practicality. Rooms are equipped with essentials such as comfortable beds, flat-screen TVs, free Wi-Fi, and mini-fridges. The décor is modern and clean, providing a cozy environment for guests.

Amenities

The hotel features a variety of amenities to enhance the guest experience. A complimentary hot breakfast is available each morning, offering a selection of breakfast items to start the day. The hotel also boasts an indoor pool and a fitness center, providing options for relaxation and exercise. Additional amenities include free parking and a business center with fax and photocopying services.

Location

Sleep Inn & Suites is conveniently located near downtown Gatlinburg, making it easy for guests to access popular attractions like the Gatlinburg SkyLift and the Great Smoky Mountains National Park. The hotel's location offers both convenience and a relatively quiet environment compared to more central accommodations.

Services

The hotel provides practical services to ensure a pleasant stay, including a 24-hour front desk and laundry facilities. The staff is attentive and available to assist with any guest needs, contributing to a positive overall experience.

Chapter 12: Dining in Gatlinburg

Local Cuisine and Specialties

Gatlinburg offers a diverse culinary landscape, blending traditional Southern fare with regional specialties. When dining in Gatlinburg, exploring the local cuisine is a must to fully experience the area's unique flavor.

Southern Comfort Food

Southern comfort food is a hallmark of Gatlinburg's dining scene. Expect hearty dishes like fried chicken, biscuits and gravy, and collard greens. These meals often feature locally sourced ingredients and are prepared with traditional Southern techniques, providing a rich, flavorful experience.

Smoky Mountain Specialties

The Smoky Mountains region is known for its rustic, hearty cuisine. Popular dishes include mountain trout, which is often pan-fried or grilled, and country ham, a staple of Appalachian cooking. Barbecue is also a favorite, with slow-cooked meats and tangy sauces that reflect the region's love for smoked and grilled flavors.

Sweet Treats

Gatlinburg is famous for its sweet treats, including homemade fudge and fresh-baked pies. Local candy shops and bakeries offer a variety of confections, from chocolate fudge to apple pie, providing a sweet finish to any meal or a tasty snack throughout the day.

Regional Ingredients

Local restaurants often incorporate regional ingredients into their dishes. Fresh mountain produce, such as apples and berries, and locally sourced meats and cheeses are commonly featured.

This emphasis on local ingredients enhances the authenticity and flavor of the cuisine.

Restaurant Recommendations

Gatlinburg boasts a variety of dining options, from casual eateries to upscale restaurants. Here are some recommendations to consider:

The Peddler Steakhouse

Known for its high-quality steaks and warm, rustic atmosphere, The Peddler Steakhouse is a popular choice for a hearty meal. The restaurant offers a selection of steak cuts, cooked to perfection, and a salad bar with fresh, seasonal ingredients.

Cherokee Grill

Cherokee Grill combines upscale dining with Southern comfort. The menu includes a variety of dishes, from steaks and seafood to pasta and salads. The restaurant's inviting atmosphere and excellent service make it a great choice for both casual and special occasions.

Gatlinburg Brewing Company

For a more relaxed dining experience, Gatlinburg Brewing Company offers a selection of craft beers brewed on-site, along with a menu of pub fare such as burgers, sandwiches, and appetizers. The casual atmosphere and live music add to the appeal of this local favorite.

Crockett's Breakfast Camp

A great spot for a hearty breakfast, Crockett's Breakfast Camp offers a range of breakfast classics, from fluffy pancakes to savory omelets. The restaurant is known for its generous portions and friendly service, making it a popular choice for starting the day off right.

Tips for Dining Out

To make the most of your dining experience in Gatlinburg, consider the following tips:

Make Reservations

Gatlinburg's popular restaurants can get busy, especially during peak tourist seasons. It's a good idea to make reservations in advance to ensure you get a table at your desired time. This is particularly important for upscale or highly recommended establishments.

Explore Local Specialties

Take the opportunity to try local specialties and regional dishes. Whether it's Southern comfort food, Smoky Mountain barbecue, or homemade desserts, exploring the local cuisine can enhance your overall dining experience and provide a taste of the area's unique flavors.

Check Reviews and Recommendations

Before dining out, check reviews and recommendations from other travelers or locals.

Websites like Yelp or TripAdvisor, as well as local guides, can provide insights into the best places to eat and help you avoid potential disappointments.

Be Prepared for Wait Times

During busy times, you may encounter wait times for popular restaurants. Be prepared for this and use the opportunity to explore nearby shops or attractions. Some restaurants also offer waiting areas or bars where you can relax while waiting for your table.

Consider Portion Sizes

Many restaurants in Gatlinburg serve generous portions, so consider sharing dishes or ordering smaller portions if you're not very hungry. This can help you try a variety of dishes without overindulging and maximize your dining experience.

Made in the USA
Las Vegas, NV
17 January 2025

16576281R00069